W9-BRY-446

RHYMES FOR ANNIE ROSE

For Elsa Madeleine

821
H

Rhymes
for
Annie Rose

SHIRLEY HUGHES

Lothrop, Lee & Shepard Books
New York

A Picture of Annie Rose

Two brown eyes,
One pink nose,
Ten busy fingers,
Ten pink toes.
Color in her brown curls,
Color in her clothes,
Color in a big smile
And that's Annie Rose.

Chirpy

All the house is quiet,
Curtains tightly drawn,
But someone sings a little song
To welcome in the dawn.

It's not time for breakfast,
Too soon to play,
But someone's very chirpy
And ready for the day.

Heads deep in pillows,
Underneath the clothes,
But all the birds are wide-awake
And so is Annie Rose.

Old Friends

There's little Teddy One Ear and Teddy Big,
Daffodil, my knitted duck, and Portly Pig,
Mr. Bones and Bonny and Raggedy Ann
And dear old Buttercup, my white woolly lamb.

Elizabeth has eyes that open and close,
Hair that you can brush and comb and very pretty clothes.
There's a white dress for a wedding and a pink one for a ball –
But I still love Buttercup best of all.

Patiently waiting, ready to play,
From when I wake up till the end of the day,
And close beside me the whole night through,
They're only toys but they're old friends too.
It would never do to tell the rest
That I love Buttercup the best.

Duck Weather

Splishing, splashing in the rain,
Up the street and back again,
Stomping, stamping through the flood,
We don't mind a bit of mud.
Running pavements, gutters flowing,
All the cars with wipers going,
We don't care about the weather,
Tramping hand in hand together.
We don't mind a damp wet day,
Sloshing puddles all the way,
Splishing, splashing in the rain,
Up the street and back again.

Teatime

Lickery, stickery, jammery jee,
Buttery toast and buns for tea.
Bears like honey and so do we,
So eat your crusts up, one, two, three.
A bite for you and a bite for me,
Lickery, stickery, jammery jee!

Bernard

I like Bernard.
Rough Bernard,
Tough Bernard,
Stop-it-that's-quite-enough Bernard,
Playing pirates, running races,
Wrinkled socks and trailing laces,
Funny jokes and wild faces,
Falling-about Bernard,
Scuffle-and-shout Bernard,
I like Bernard.

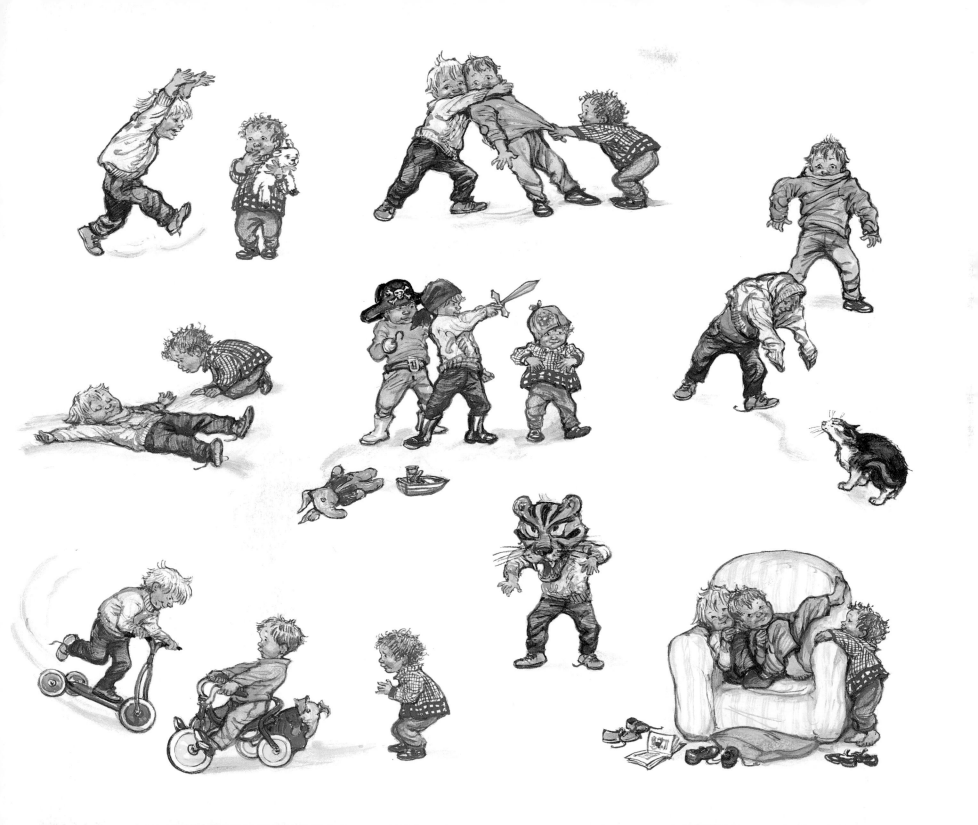

Footprints

We went out, and in the night
All the world had turned to white.
Snowy garden, snowy hedge,
Ice along the window ledge.
And all around the garden seat
A tiny bird with tiny feet
Had left his footprints in the snow,
As he went hopping to and fro.

Teeny Tiny

A stocking full of presents,
Open each with care,
A toy watch and a shiny ball,
A chocolate teddy bear,
And something at the bottom
That I never knew was there –
A teeny tiny dolly
With bright yellow hair.

She wears a teeny tiny dress,
A teeny tiny wrap,
And teeny tiny shoes to match
Her teeny tiny cap.
I'll keep her in my pocket,
Look after her with care,
My teeny tiny dolly
With the bright yellow hair.

Mouse?

Tick, tock, dickory dock,
Where is the mouse
Who ran down the clock?
I've looked in the cupboard,

In Elizabeth's bed
And under the chair,
But he isn't there.

I've looked on the stair,

No hint of a whisker,
No wriggly pink nose,
Where has he gone to?
Nobody knows.
Tick, tock, dickory dock,
Oh, where is the mouse
Who ran down the clock?

Night Flight

Annie flew out of the window,
Bedclothes and crib and all,
And floated around above the ground,
And over the garden wall.

And her shadow skimmed over the gardens
And followed her all the way,
As she looked down on the roofs of the town
And the moon shone as bright as day.

Fingers

One little finger
Dancing on her own,
Joined by another one,
Now she's not alone.
Up jumps the middle one,
Strong and tall,

Here comes the fourth one,
Liveliest of all.
Stubby old Tom Thumb
Has nowhere to go,
Put him with the others
And there's five in a row.

Toes

Beatie Bo,
Big toe.
Mrs. Moore,
Next door.
Solomon Riddle,
In the middle.
Lucky Jim,
Next to him.
And last of all,
Curled up small,
Fat little Billy Ball.

JOHN H. FULLER SCHOOL
LIBRARY/MEDIA CENTER

Houses

Come around to my house,
Knock at the door,
And we'll have a tea party
Sitting on the floor.

I'll come to your house,
Bring a friend as well,
Tap at the window,
Ring at the bell.

You can stay at my house,
Just for a treat.
I'll give you lots of fizzy drinks
And lovely things to eat.

I could come to your house,
Visit you instead.
I could stay forever –
Or till it's time for bed.

The Knobbly Tree

The knobbly tree
Is wider than me,
With a secret place
Where it's safe to be.
A hollow you can creep inside,
A sort of room where you can hide.
And no one can see
Alfie and me
When we're snug as two bugs
In the knobbly tree.

Bedtime *(with salutations to A.A.Milne)*

What is the matter with Annie Rose?
Nothing would please her today.
She wouldn't have stories or sit on my lap,
She was far too bad-tempered to play.
Lunchtime was awful, quite a disgrace –
Carrots and gravy all over the place!
And when did you ever see such a cross face?
She wasn't her best today.

But now that it's nearly time for bed,
She's having a change of mood.
She built me a castle and sang me a song
And chatted and laughed and cooed.
She ate up her supper and asked for some more,
No bits of banana or crust on the floor,
She's the best-behaved person that I ever saw –
What can have made her so good?

Shipwreck

Little wooden sailor,
Brand-new boat.
Take them to the pond
And set them afloat.

Makes a large tidal wave
Shaped like a V,
Very choppy weather
Far out at sea.

Wind begins to carry them
Far from the beach,
Jauntily sailing
Way out of reach.
Fine white daddy duck
Decides to take a swim,
Waddles to the water,
Lunges in.

Catches little sailor
Quite by surprise –
Boat and captain
Both capsize!
Nearly underwater,
Bobbing up and down.
Will the boat go under?
Will the sailor drown?

Dog to the rescue
Right up to her neck,
Strikes out bravely
Straight for the wreck.

Dog lands sailor,
Gives a big grin.
Shaggy coat, sopping wet,
Long dripping ears,
Looks about, pleased as punch,
Everybody cheers.
Boat and sailor
Both safe and sound.
Dog gives her coat a shake
And soaks us all around!

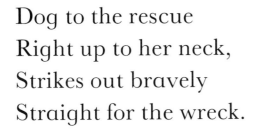

Head above water,
Paddling with her paws,
Takes the wooden sailor
Safely in her jaws.
Someone finds a long stick,
Hauls the boat in.

Girlfriends

Marian, Lily, and Annie Rose
Are three bonny girls, as everyone knows.
Sometimes bouncy, sometimes sad,
Sometimes sleepy, sometimes glad,
Sometimes grubby, sometimes clean,
Often kind, though sometimes mean.
But most of the time they try to be good,
And to all who know them it's understood
That Marian, Lily, and Annie Rose
Are best of friends, as everyone knows.

The Garden Path

The garden path at Grandma's
Leads past the little pond,
Where nimble golden fishes hide,
To tunneled leaves beyond.

And through the jungly bit you find
A gate beside a tree,
And a huge world made of grass and sky
As far as you can see.

The End of the Bed

Curl up tight and bury your head,
What's down there at the end of the bed?
Screw up your eyes or you might see
The Thing at the bottom where your feet ought to be.

The Snickering Snapper in his underground lair,
The Pebble-Eyed Wobbler with the jelly-green hair,
The humped-up creature that you're quite sure is there,
Deep down dark at the end of the bed –
Quick! Lie quite still and pretend you're dead!

Feet

Riding in the stroller
On a busy street,
All I see are shopping bags
And other people's feet.

If the bus is crowded
And we haven't got a seat,
I'm sandwiched in between
the knees
And other people's feet.

When grown-ups ask their friends in,
All I get to meet
Are lots of different trouser legs
And shiny party feet.

But if I'm riding piggyback
Holding very tight,
I see hats and faces,
tops of heads,
And not a foot in sight.

Cows

Cows graze,
Slowly turn their heads to gaze,
With twitching ears and soft brown eyes,
And swishy tails for swishing flies.
Chewing, mooing, chomping grass,
Slowly through the field they pass.
All the lazy summer days,
Cows graze.

Summer Numbers

Ten tall aerials, pointing at the sky,
Nine brown birds, swooping by,
Eight parked cars, baking in the street,
Seven pretty flowerpots, lined up neat,
Six hot schoolboys, trailing home late,
Five friendly neighbors, chatting by the gate,
Four lazy cats, sitting in the shade,
Three laughing ladies, sipping lemonade,
Two squealing children, playing with the hose,
One of them is Alfie and the other's –
Annie Rose!

Monday Morning Dance

Dungarees and nighties, underpants and socks,
Alfie's dirty T-shirts, Annie Rose's frocks –
Tip them in a heap from the overflowing bin,
Pick them up and sort them out and bundle them in.
Shove them in and switch it on and make them turn around,
Make them turn round and round and round,
Make them turn round and round.

Through the little window, you can see the dancing shirts,
Pajama bottoms waltzing with Annie Rose's skirts,
Colored tights and trousers, stepping out and in,
Leaping in the bubbles of an ever wilder spin,
And even odd socks wonder if a partner can be found,
As the washing goes round and round and round,
As the washing goes round and round.

Castles

Annie built a castle
Right up to the sky,
With a clock on top to tell the time
For people passing by.

She built another castle
Of sand, one summer's day,
But in the end a wave came up
And washed it all away.

One Winter Evening

One winter evening, time for bed,
One winter evening late,
We heard a bird with a breast of red
Sing by the garden gate.

He cocked his head with its bright black eye
And sang in the still damp air,
And a star came out in a pale yellow sky
And silently twinkled there.

Sea Voyagers

A pool of lapping lamplight,
A cushion for a boat,
The floor is made of water
And we are both afloat.

Steep behind the sofa
The darkened caverns gloom.
Steer between the dripping cliffs,
Hear the ocean boom.

If we can reach the island
In the middle of the floor,
We could pull our boats up
On a shallow shore.

Light a fire of driftwood,
Cast our lines of string,
Try to catch a flying fish
Or hear a mermaid sing.

Don't go near the table cave,
For there beneath the stones,
The sea monster is stirring
On his bed of bones.

We'll have to go the long way round
Beyond the farthest flood,
Where many wrecks lie grounded
On the banks of mud.

Row among the chair rocks
Around the lighthouse stool,
Back to port and safety
In our lighted pool.

Lullaby

Time for sleep, time to rest,
Snuggle in your woolly nest.
Let me safely tuck you in,
Dark without, warm within.

Far away, train whistles call,
Car lights sweep the nursery wall,
Muffled footsteps passing by,
A quiet moon in a quiet sky.

Soft blanket, smooth sheet,
Tuck the quilt around your feet,
Close your eyes and I will keep
A watch beside you while you sleep.

13.60   9/96

Copyright © 1995 by Shirley Hughes
First published in Great Britain by The Bodley Head.
All rights reserved. No part of this book may be reproduced or utilized in any form or by any means, electronic or mechanical,
including photocopying and recording, or by any information storage and retrieval system,
without permission in writing from the Publisher. Inquiries should be addressed to
Lothrop, Lee & Shepard Books, a division of William Morrow & Company, Inc.,
1350 Avenue of the Americas, New York, New York 10019.
Printed in Hong Kong

First U.S. Edition   1 2 3 4 5 6 7 8 9 10
Library of Congress Cataloging in Publication Data
Hughes, Shirley.
Rhymes for Annie Rose / Shirley Hughes.
p. cm.
Summary: A collection of more than twenty poems about young
Annie Rose and the daily activities of a child.
ISBN 0-688-14220-6
1. Children's poetry, English. [1. English poetry.] I. Title.
PR6058.U368R49 1995 821'.914—dc20 94-37544 CIP AC